St. Wulfram's church in the middle of Grantham began life as a Saxo
rebuilt in the 1100s. It was the first of many changes.

What has emerged from these additions, modifications and embellish
decorative, gives us a church of cathedral proportions set in precincts
elegance which has inspired craftsmen in stone, glass, wood and texti

The booklet is a tribute to their inspiration, and a guide to the visitors to the church to find and
appreciate the many - though sometimes well hidden
- gems that the church contains. Some items are not
always on display and it may be necessary to make an
appointment to view them.

INDEX

Many photographs contain a position
indicator which identifies the location of the
item and is marked in the plan of the church
at the back of the booklet. They also refer to
the book *The Parish Church of St. Wulfram,
Grantham* in the Francis Trigge Library
referenced earlier.

A plan of the church showing the main architectural features

A version of this plan included at the end of the booklet shows the location of many of the images that follow.

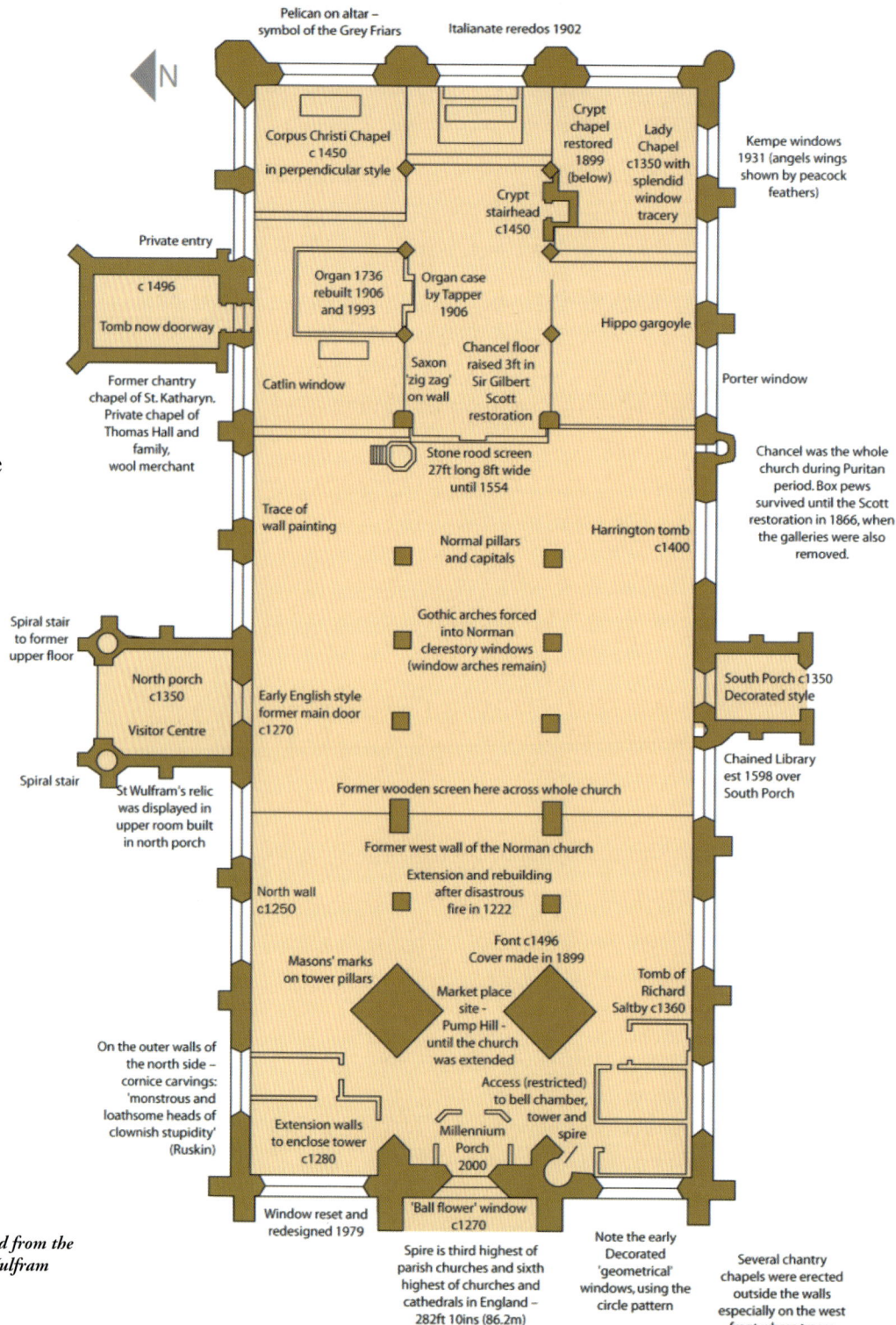

N

Pelican on altar – symbol of the Grey Friars

Italianate reredos 1902

Corpus Christi Chapel c1450 in perpendicular style

Crypt chapel restored 1899 (below)

Lady Chapel c1350 with splendid window tracery

Kempe windows 1931 (angels wings shown by peacock feathers)

Private entry

c1496

Tomb now doorway

Crypt stairhead c1450

Organ 1736 rebuilt 1906 and 1993

Organ case by Tapper 1906

Hippo gargoyle

Former chantry chapel of St. Katharyn. Private chapel of Thomas Hall and family, wool merchant

Catlin window

Saxon 'zig zag' on wall

Chancel floor raised 3ft in Sir Gilbert Scott restoration

Porter window

Stone rood screen 27ft long 8ft wide until 1554

Chancel was the whole church during Puritan period. Box pews survived until the Scott restoration in 1866, when the galleries were also removed.

Trace of wall painting

Normal pillars and capitals

Harrington tomb c1400

Spiral stair to former upper floor

Gothic arches forced into Norman clerestory windows (window arches remain)

North porch c1350

Visitor Centre

Early English style former main door c1270

South Porch c1350 Decorated style

Chained Library est 1598 over South Porch

Spiral stair

St Wulfram's relic was displayed in upper room built in north porch

Former wooden screen here across whole church

Former west wall of the Norman church

North wall c1250

Extension and rebuilding after disastrous fire in 1222

Font c1496 Cover made in 1899

Masons' marks on tower pillars

Market place site – Pump Hill – until the church was extended

Tomb of Richard Saltby c1360

On the outer walls of the north side – cornice carvings: 'monstrous and loathsome heads of clownish stupidity' (Ruskin)

Access (restricted) to bell chamber, tower and spire

Extension walls to enclose tower c1280

Millennium Porch 2000

Window reset and redesigned 1979

'Ball flower' window c1270

Note the early Decorated 'geometrical' windows, using the circle pattern

Several chantry chapels were erected outside the walls especially on the west front where traces can be seen.

Spire is third highest of parish churches and sixth highest of churches and cathedrals in England – 282ft 10ins (86.2m)

diagram by Geoff Horsfall reprinted from the booklet The Parish Church of St.Wulfram

1

A short history

When the Domesday Book was prepared in 1086 Grantham was a Saxon settlement with a population of over 1000 people. There was a stone Saxon church dedicated to St. Wulfram which had an annual income of 100 shillings. Wulfram was elected Archbishop of Sens in 692, and resigned three years later to become a missionary to the Frisians. He died in 720 and his remains were eventually buried in the church of Notre Dame in Abbeville.

Queen Edith, wife of Edward the Confessor (1042 - 1066), may well have been given some relics of the saint which were deposited at Grantham in a church which was then named after him. In 1566 it is recorded that a silver and copper shrine called the 'Saint Wulfram shrine' (probably containing the relic of the saint) was sold as part of Elizabeth I's policy to establish and order the Church of England.

In the 1100s, a Norman church was built on the site of the Saxon church, forming the kernel of the present church. This church had a nave the same width as today's and was 140 feet long. Six of the original pillars still remain and would have had rounded arches. Traces of the original rounded Norman arches for the clerestory can still be seen in the nave walls.

The big expansion to give the church its current footprint took place in 1280 - 1380, leaving just the addition of St. Kathryn's chapel (now the Clergy Vestry) to be added in c1496. The glorious sight of the west front and the soaring spire, the tallest in the country when it was built at 282 ft 10 in. (86.2m), was complete.

By the middle of the 18th century the church had been divided into two parts by a wooden screen partially glazed and housing the Byfield organ. There was a bachelors' gallery in the north aisle and the floor of the church was divided irregularly by family pews. In 1863, George Gilbert Scott, a Victorian church architect of national fame, was asked to recommend a plan for the restoration of the inside of the church.

His proposal gives us the plan and appearance of the inside of the church as it is today. The screen dividing the chancel from the nave, the reredos and the siting of the organ date from this time; as does the re-siting of some of the memorials to the north and south walls and the removal of the family pews, gallery and glass screen and most of the woodwork.

It also resulted in the removal of the plaster covering of the interior walls which in medieval times would have been richly decorated with colourful designs, symbols, biblical scenes and characters.

In 2014 a major reconstruction of the upper third of the spire had to be undertaken, This shows the spire, its glory smothered in scaffolding.

photo by Roger Graves

Window Tracery

The window styles and tracery of St. Wulfram's span a period of architectural development from 1200 to 1500.

C. Early English Style, Geometric Tracery

H. Early English Style, Intersecting Tracery

P. Decorated Style, Flowing Tracery

S. Perpendicular Style and Tracery

U. Decorated Style, Reticulated Tracery

Stained Glass

The stained glass in St. Wulfram's is mainly Victorian with modern additions by L C Evetts, John Hayward & Harry Harvey.

There are five windows designed by a famous Victorian designer Charles Kempe (1837 - 1907) and his firm.

Q. The Glaister Window
designed by C E Kempe & Co.
Installed 1920
'The Incarnation'

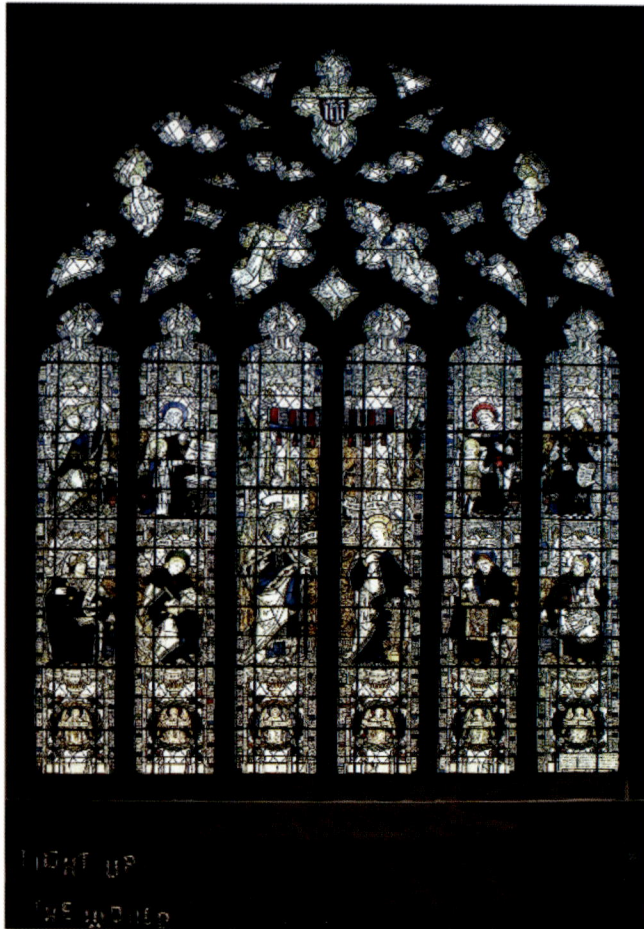

N. The Porter Window
designed by L C Evetts 1969 showing the Son of God descending at the Incarnation, and the offering to God of our lives and our work

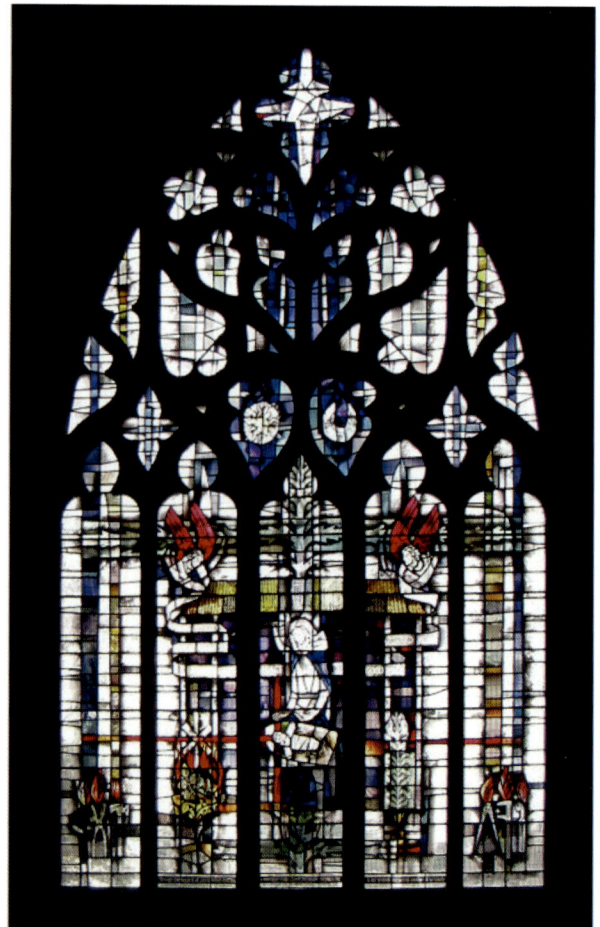

Stone Heads

There are over 700 stone heads inside and outside the church. Their age is difficult to determine but probably medieval. The subject matter is sometimes natural, sometimes grotesque and sometimes bestial. Some of the heads are very small; those on the pinnacles over the crypt stairhead inside the church are probably no more than a 3 cm cube. (see 138 below)

The heads outside the church are exposed to the elements and greatly eroded.

A catalogue of the heads exists in *The Parish Church of St. Wulfram, Grantham* (480) in the Francis Trigge Library.

Heads inside the church

90

34

113

138

142

104

64

24

40 Dragon eating tail

6

Heads outside the church

The windows are labelled A to X in the plan at the back of the booklet. The heads on this page are identified by their window letter and position from the left.

A12 ↑

F14

← B13

A01

A13

H. one of many 'ball flowers'

A04

M02

A06

H10

C11

F02

K18

F24

F15

The Francis Trigge chained library

In 1598 the Revd. Francis Trigge, Rector of Welbourn, arranged for a library to be provided in St. Wulfram's church, Grantham, for the use of the clergy and inhabitants of the town and 'soke' (i.e. a minor administrative district); Trigge undertook to supply books to the value of 'one hundereth poundes or thereabouts' perhaps worth £20,000 in 2018 terms. This was the first English library to be endowed under a civic authority, in this case the Borough of Grantham, rather than belonging to a cathedral, church, college or school. Isaac Newton, who was a pupil 1655 - 1660 at the King's School next door to St. Wulfram's, may well have used the library as the schoolmaster was one of the four keyholders.

It is probable that Trigge sent an agent to Cambridge to buy the books. It would appear from the range of books purchased that the agent bought what was easily available up to the prescribed amount. In the process he acquired a number of works on divinity and some others of more general interest (e.g. medicine, animals, geography, history) as well as a number of obscure legal works.

The initial purchase provided around 300 books, the books being chained to the presses. At a cost of several hundred pounds a book in today's terms, each book was valuable and being open to access by the public, very necessary to be secured - hence the chains. In due course these were housed in the upper floor of the South Porch.

One of three book cases in the Trigge library. It was quite normal for books to be printed separately and the binding done later. So the title was often written on the open edge. Once bound they were placed on the shelf with the spine at the back. This also avoided the books being twisted or damaged when pulled out to view the title.

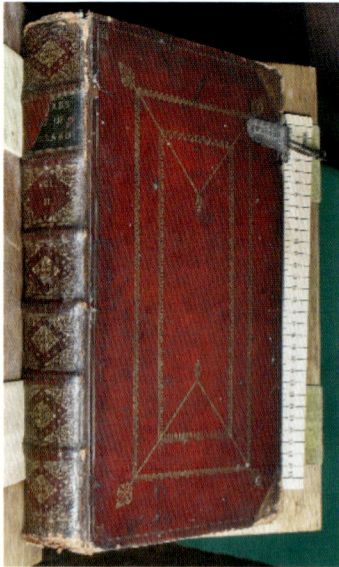

106. Showing the chain fastening to the book end cover publ. 1718

202. This is the oldest book in the library printed in Venice and is a collection of legal judgements. publ. 1472

Moveable type printing was first recorded in China around 1040 AD, and in Europe Gutenberg working in Mainz printed his first Bible using this technology in 1455. From Mainz the technology spread to Venice and Paris where Caxton was working. Caxton set up his first press in Westminster in 1476.

Some of the books were quite old when Trigge bought them in 1598. Books printed before 1501 are known as 'incunabula', and there are seven books of this age in the library.

The earliest book (202) was published in 1472 and the newest (480) in 2014. A digital catalogue does exist and the references above - 202 and 480 - refer to this catalogue. An index of the books referred to here is given at the end of the booklet.

Many physical bindings may contain several different books published at different times - 202 is such an example, with two important publications included at the end - important because the first is the only known copy in the world, and the second is one of only two - both published in 1476.

The end of the 15th century was a turbulent time. In Britain it was the War of the Roses, in Europe the time of the Spanish inquisition and the rise of protestantism. Creating a collection of books printed in Germany, France and Venice and setting up a library in a small market town was an amazing event.

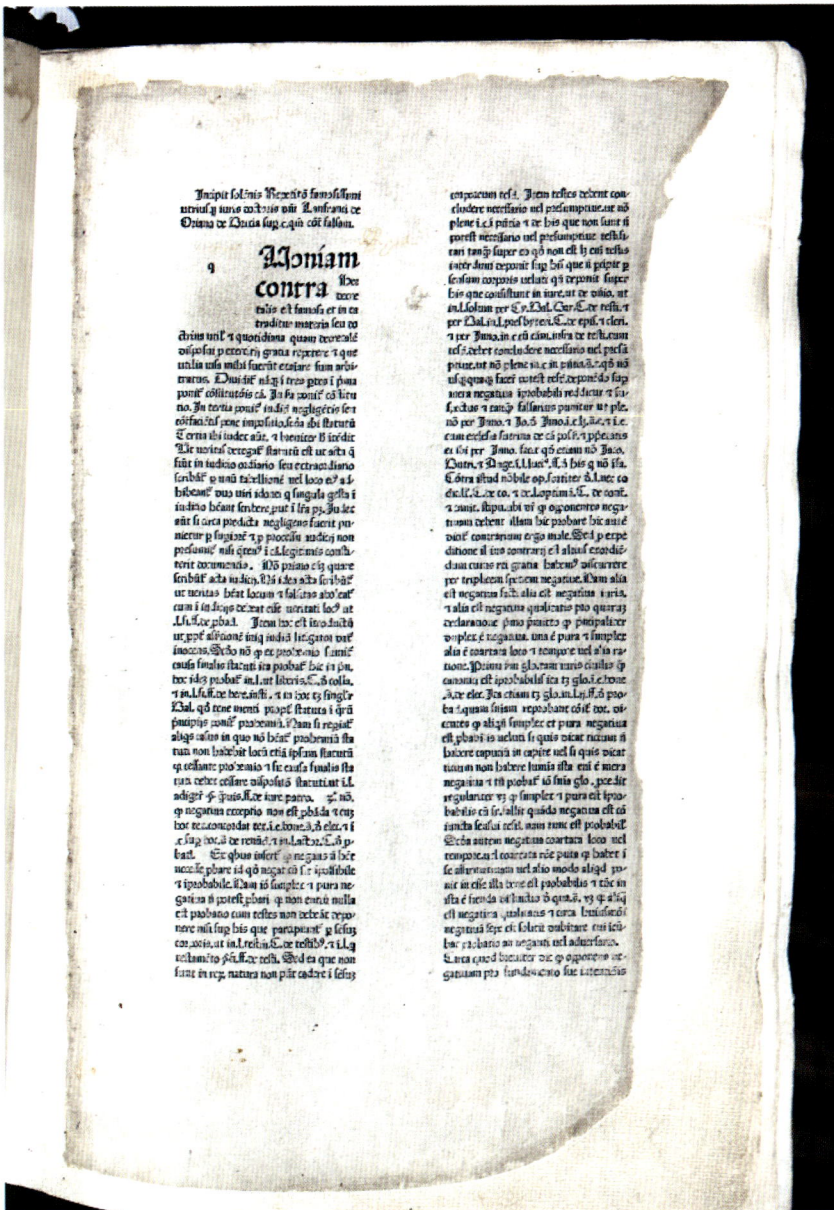

202. A page from the earliest book publ. 1472

Below is an enlarged fragment to show the Gothic typeface as developed by Gutenberg.

Later printers modified this to make it more legible, thus creating the Roman typeface which then became the standard.

The example below is from 063. publ. 1583

These two images record the change in our knowledge of the geography of Earth, the first (004) published in 1483 and the second (174) in 1656.

004. Map of the World publ. 1483

Many copies of this book were printed. One copy held in the Seville Cathedral Library inspired Christopher Columbus to set out to discover America in 1492.

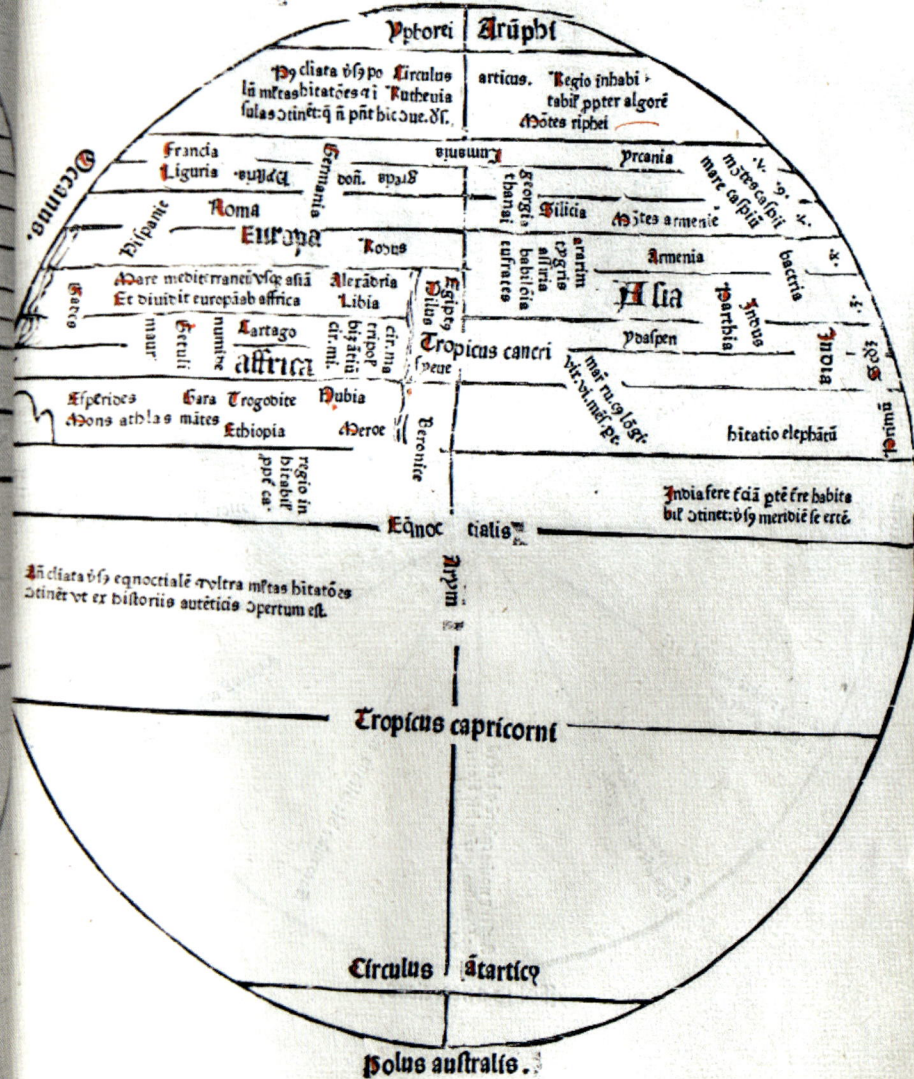

174. Map of Africa taken from the Imago Mundi

The map is in a book published in 1656. Together with three other books it is bound in leather as a single volume. This binding practice is typical of the period.

152. The images on this page all come from the same Bestiary which is in 2 volumes. publ. 1597

De Vlula. Lib.III. 775

DE VPVPA.

↑ 152.1. An owl

152.2. A camel →

152.2. A unicorn →

Monocerote. A. Lib. I. 781

DE MONOCEROTE

PAN VEL SATYRVS MARINVS.

← 152.1. A merman

ICONEM hanc ichthyocentauri, siue dæmonis marini, ut ita dicam, à pictore quodam olim accepi qui talis monstri sceleton Antuerpiæ depictu se accepisse aiebat. Alius etiam retulit simile monstrum aridum è Noruegia in Germaniã inferiorem aduectum, marem & fœminã. Fidem ei

Most of the books in the Trigge Library are principally of interest to people studying divinity. Apart from sermons, commentaries and prayer books there are some very interesting bibles. In the 4th century, Jerome produced a bible in Latin - the Vulgate bible - which became the standard bible for the Roman Catholic world for many centuries.

The Trigge library was set up in 1598, which was at the end of two centuries of explosive interest in religion. This was driven by the growth in protestantism, the translation of the bible into English, and the invention of the printing press. The bible translations passed through four major versions of which the Trigge library has two.

Great Bible first published 1539. - A product of the Reformation - was the first authorised bible in English. Around 9000 copies had been printed by 1541, mostly in London.

Geneva Bible first published 1560. - It was the first bible to be mechanically printed in English and thus to be made available to a very wide population to buy. It used the new 'Roman' type instead of the old Gothic or 'black letter' type, making the text much more readable (see p.10).

It was the primary bible of the protestant movement in the 16th century, and would have been familiar to Shakespeare, Donne and Bunyan. It was the bible carried by the Pilgrim Fathers to America in 1620.

However it leant heavily on its Calvinistic origins and thus of Presbyterianism. The Presbyterians wanted the church to be governed by lay people not Bishops.

Bishops' Bible publ. 1568. It was based on the Geneva translations with the offending Calvinistic elements removed.

King James Bible first published 1611. James I commissioned and then authorised this version for use in the Church of England. It comprises the Old and New Testaments and the Book of Psalms. This edition was to be the dominant bible used for the next three centuries. An image of a copy in the Trigge library is on page 16 (406).

47. Title page from a Geneva bible publ. 1599

Most books up to about the mid 17th century were written in Latin. Some scholarly books were written in two or three languages. The extract below is from 039, a 'polyglot' bible printed in Antwerp in several volumes c. 1573 and has a column for Latin (the Vulgate version), Greek and a translation of the Greek into Latin.

LIBER SAPIENTIAE.

Translat. B. Hierony.

CAP. I.

Diligite iustitiã, q iudicatis terram. Sentite de Dño in bonitate, & in simplicitate cordis querite illú. ‡ Quoniã inuenitur ab his qui nõ tentatillú; apparet autẽ eis qui fidẽ habent in illú. ‡ Per⸗

ΣΟΦΙΑ ΣΑΛΟΜΩΝΤΟΣ

κεφ. α.

Γαπήσαle τὼ δικαιο- σύω oi κẽίνοντες τὴυ γλũ᷍ φεγνήσαte πεεì τõ κυρίẽ ἐν ἀγαθό- τητι, ἐν ἁπλότητι καρ δίας ζητήσατε αὐτόν.
‡ ὅτι εὑρίσκε⸗) τõῖς μὴ πειεάζẽσιν αὐτόν, ἐμφανίζε⸗) ʒ τõῖς μὴ ἀπισõõσιν

Interp. Græc.

CAP. I.

Diligite iustitiam qui iudicatis terram: sentite de Domino in bonitate, ʒ in simplicitate cordis que⸗ ‡ rite illú. ‡ Quoniã inuenitur ab his qui non tentant illú, appa⸗

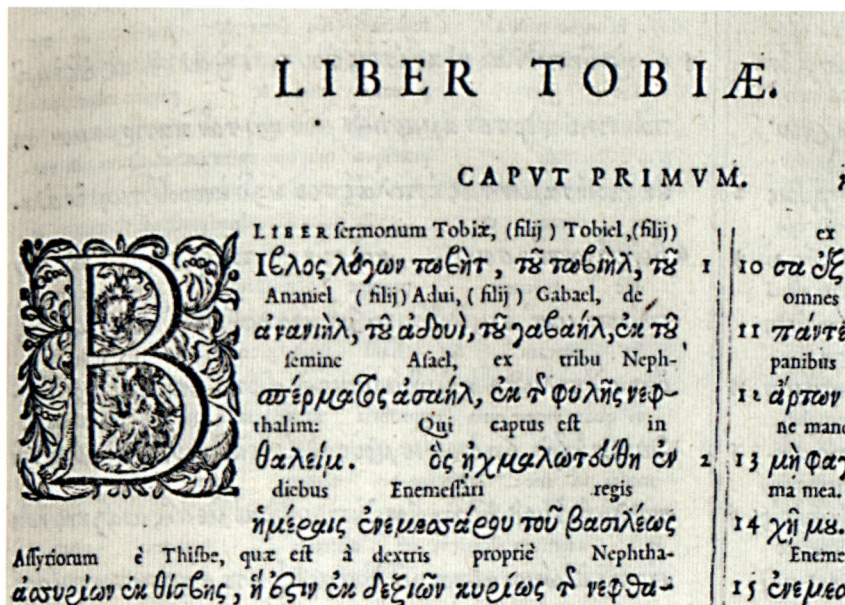

LIBER TOBIÆ.

CAPVT PRIMVM.

Liber sermonum Tobiæ, (filij) Tobiel,(filij)
Ιελος λόγων τõβῆτ, τõ τõβιὴλ, τõ
Ananiel (filij) Adui, (filij) Gabael, de
ἀνανιὴλ, τõ ἀδυὶ, τõ γαβαὴλ, ἐκ τõ
semine Asael, ex tribu Neph-
σπέρματõς ἀσαὴλ, ἐκ ᷁ φυλῆς νεφ-
thalim: Qui captus est in
θαλείμ. ὃς ἠχμαλωτόθη ἐν
diebus Enemessar regis
ἡμέραις ἐνεμεσσάρõυ τõ βασιλέως
Assyriorum è Thisbe, quæ est à dextris propriè Nephtha-
ἀσσυρίων ἐκ θίσβης, ἥ ὅςιν ἐκ δεξιῶν κυρίως ᷁ νεφθα-

		ex
	10	σα ᷂ξ omnes
	11	πάντε panibus
	12	ἄρτων ne mand
	13	μὴ φαγ ma mea.
	14	χῖ μẽ. Enemel
	15	ἐνεμεσ

040. Detail of a polyglot bible publ. 1584

showing a Latin translation of the Greek and the Greek version below each line

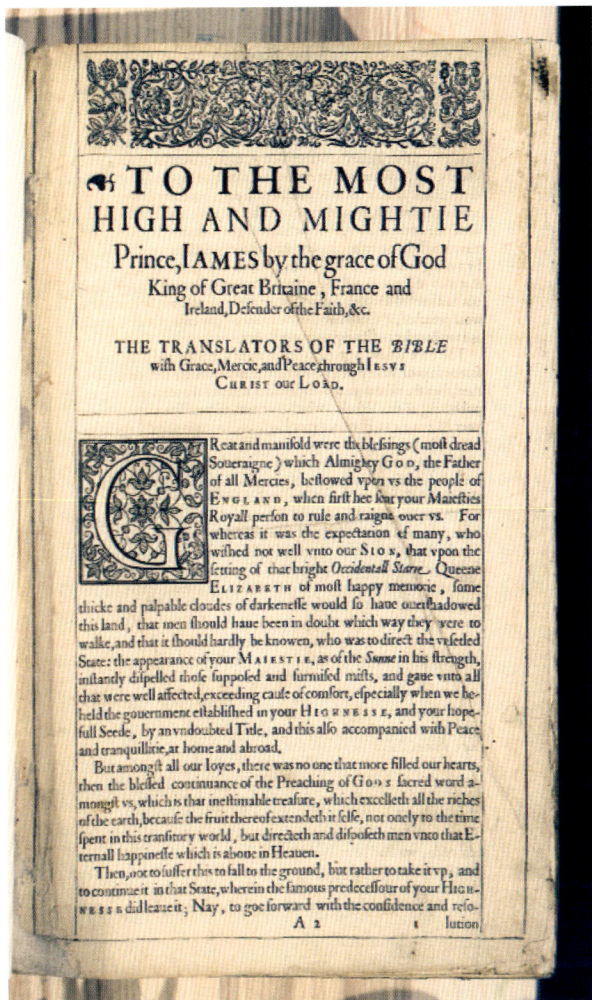

TO THE MOST HIGH AND MIGHTIE Prince, IAMES by the grace of God King of Great Britaine, France and Ireland, Defender of the Faith, &c.

THE TRANSLATORS OF THE *BIBLE* with Grace, Mercie, and Peace, through IESVS CHRIST our LORD.

Reat and manifold were the blessings (most dread Soueraigne) which Almighty GOD, the Father of all Mercies, bestowed vpon vs the people of ENGLAND, when first hee sent your Maiesties Royall person to rule and raigne ouer vs. For whereas it was the expectation of many, who wished not well vnto our SION, that vpon the setting of that bright *Occidentall Starre*, Queene ELIZABETH of most happy memorie, some thicke and palpable cloudes of darkenesse would so haue ouershadowed this land, that men should haue been in doubt which way they were to walke, and that it should hardly be knowen, who was to direct the vnsetled State: the appearance of your MAIESTIE, as of the *Sunne* in his strength, instantly dispelled those supposed and surmised mists, and gaue vnto all that were well affected, exceeding cause of comfort, especially when we beheld the gouernment established in your HIGHNESSE, and your hopefull Seede, by an vndoubted Title, and this also accompanied with Peace and tranquillitie, at home and abroad.

But amongst all our ioyes, there was no one that more filled our hearts, then the blessed continuance of the Preaching of GODS sacred word amongst vs, which is that inestimable treasure, which excelleth all the riches of the earth, because the fruit thereof extendeth it selfe, not onely to the time spent in this transitory world, but directeth and disposeth men vnto that Eternall happinesse which is aboue in Heauen.

Then, not to suffer this to fall to the ground, but rather to take it vp, and to continue it in that State, wherein the famous predecessour of your HIGHNESSE did leaue it; Nay, to goe forward with the confidence and reso-

A 2   lution.

406. Dedication page to a King James bible publ. 1613

Note that there is no J in this alphabet, nor U or W.

041. Manuscript fragment dating from the 15th century with musical staves and words from a service for Candlemas, from a *Manuale* also extant in the 'Rathen Manual' used by the Scottish church before the Reformation, and referred to in the Arbuthnot Missal (cf. Duncan MacGregor, *The Rathen Manual* (Aberdeen, 1905)).
Pasted into Pars Seconda: Iosue - Hester a Biblia Latina.
The host book was published 1507.

051. English bible incl. Psalms, Old and New Testaments publ. 1717

Some books are very large (051 The Holy Bible publ. 1716) and some very small (405 also a Holy Bible with Old and New Testaments). The smallest (439) only has simple devotional pictures.

051. Measures
564 x 364 mm

405

439

← 405. And with pictures measures 42 x 30 mm

439. ↓ Measures 30 x 24 mm

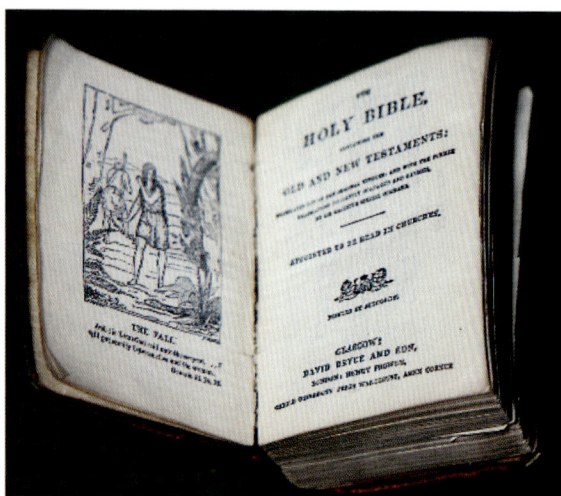

Textiles

The Altar frontals, vestments and banners date from Victorian times up to today. Of all the adornments and decorations in the church they are the most susceptible to wear and tear.

They are also well worth close inspection to appreciate the skill and artistry of the embroiderer.

The middle angel

Choir of Angels frontal

made by Watts & Co to a design by William Morris or possibly Sir William Tapper

donated in 1920 by Annie Hutchinson and others

The frontal shows twelve names in Latin of the Virgin Mary mostly drawn from the Litany of Loreto with appropriate images.

from left to right depicting the Virgin as:

> 'the spring of eternal life'
> 'the Gateway to Heaven'
> 'the Queen of Angels'

Fons hortoru̅

Porta ✠ Cœli

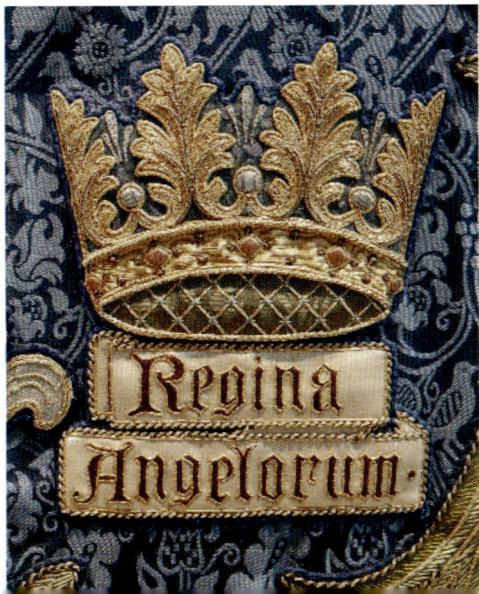

Blessed Virgin Mary Frontal made by Watts & Co. to a design by Sir Walter Tapper

donated by Emma Sedgwick in 1924

Enlarged angel's face

Detail from the Green
and Gold chasuble

Green and Gold chasuble c. 1880

Detail from the Green chasuble

Green chasuble designed and
made by Mary Sleigh 2000 to
go with the Green frontal on
p.27

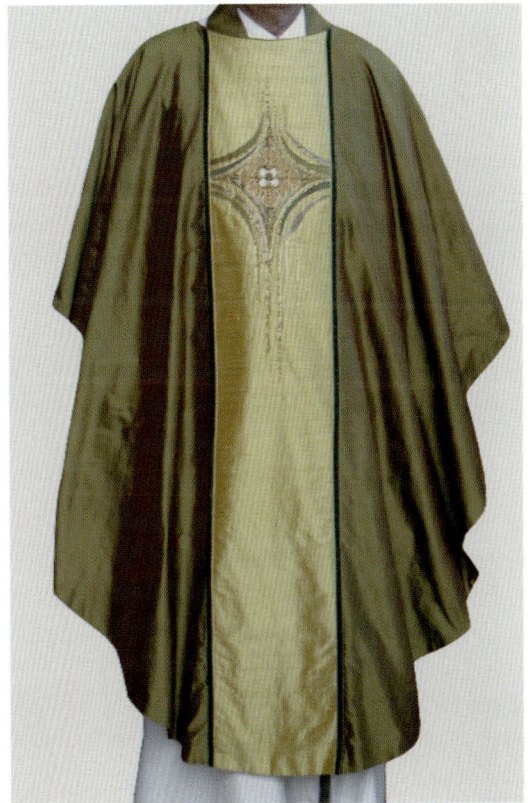

Saint's Day frontal (red) on prior page
designed by Charles Kempe

donated by the parishioners of the church in 1887

Details of the Saint's Day (red) frontal

The centre panel of the Red altar frontal shows the wear caused by the priest when he stood in front of the altar during the Communion service facing east.

Photo was taken September 2013.

Detail from the Red altar frontal →

Detail from the super frontal for the Red altar frontal ↓

Green altar frontal designed by Sir Walter Tapper 1923

VERBVM CARO FACCVM ESC EC HABICAVIC IN NOBIS

Nativity detail

Crucifixion detail

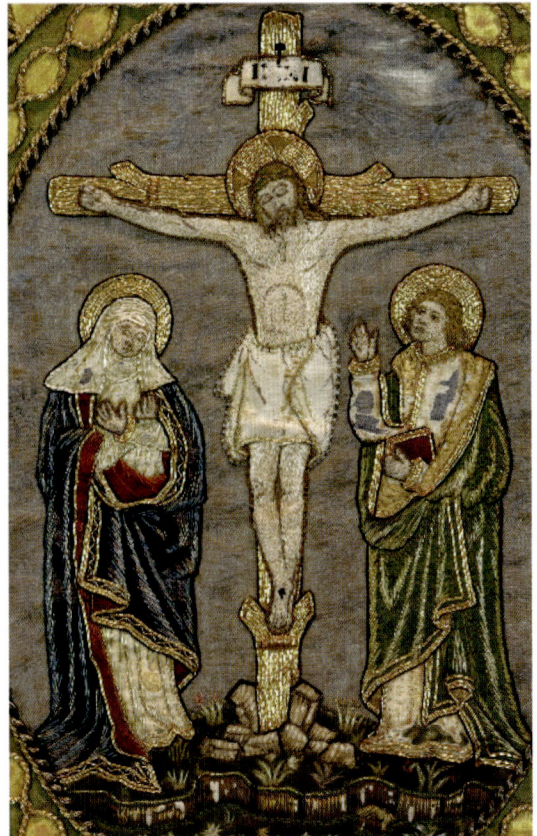

Wooden Carvings

Only two pieces of ancient wood work survived the destruction that came with the Civil War and the Restoration. The two chests (p.35) were used to store the church plate and the larger one, the 'Common Hutch', stored the borough charters and other important documents.

All the other decorative and free standing woodwork was destroyed at the time of the Civil War in 1643. The present roof including the organ case, the friezes in the north and south aisles, the inscription in the nave and chancel, and the angels date from the Gilbert Scott re-ordering of the church in the late 19th century. The woodwork existing at the re-ordering was stripped out and sold or destroyed.

The friezes, where the roof meets the stone walls, in the north and south aisles consist of carvings of mostly mythical or fictional beasts including dragons, lizards, snakes, birds, dogs, pigs and a green man. There are at least 100 carvings. They are very difficult to see without special lighting and binoculars.

The plan at the end of the booklet gives approximate locations for each image.

1162. A dragon - N aisle N wall

1212. A lizard
N aisle N wall

1493. A green man
S aisle N wall

1424. A pair of phoenix
N aisle N wall

1199. A winged lion ↑ - N aisle S wall

1456. A pair of stoats ↓ - S aisle S wall

1569. A dog S aisle S wall

1573. A bird S aisle S wall

In the choir stalls (1868) in the chancel there are some fine
pew ends and mythical beasts carved on the arm rests.

The oak lectern was given in
memory of William Carr Smith
who was vicar of Grantham 1910
- 1917 and who died in 1930. On
top is a fine carving of St.
Wulfram in his Archbishop's
robes.

Bishops' chairs with a detail of
an arm rest to the left

The wooden font cover on top of the 15th century stone font was made in 1899 to celebrate Queen Victoria's Diamond Jubilee. It has three carved figures of Edward the Confessor, St. Hugh of Lincoln and St. Wulfram.

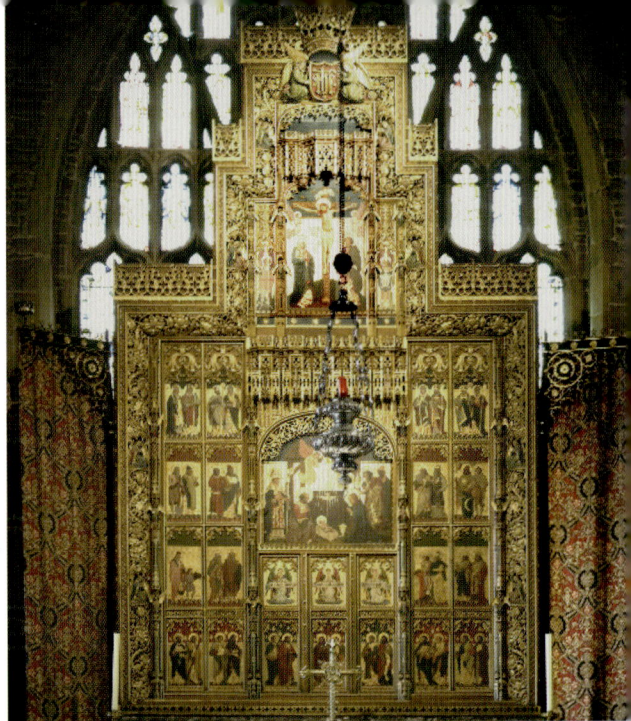

The reredos was designed by Sir Arthur C. Blomfield in 1883 and extended by Sir Walter Tapper in 1901/2.

Detail from the middle of the reredos showing the Adoration by the Magi of the Christ child

St. Hugh of Lincoln

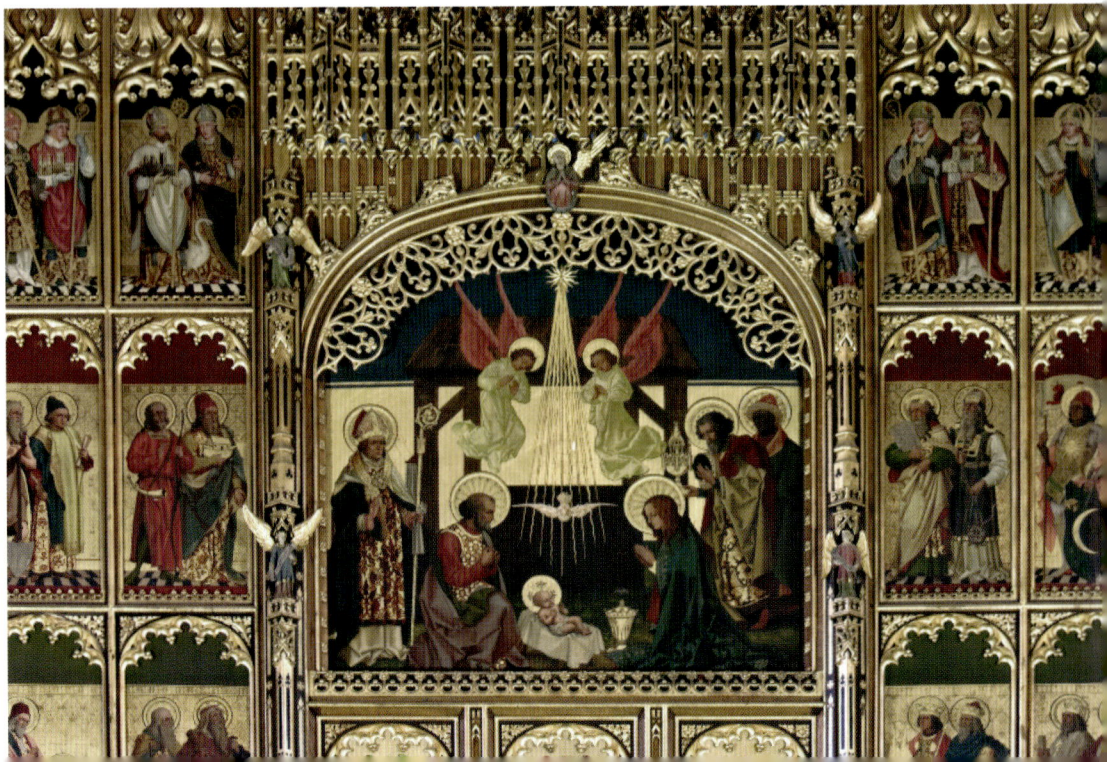

The pulpit carries a dedication in memory of Richard Cust 1869.

In the nave and chancel there are 22 wooden, carved and decorated angels installed as part of the frieze.

There are a further 56 undecorated angels in the friezes of the north and south aisles.

170

Detail of a panel on the side of the pulpit

There are six hatchments and three coats of
arms on the south wall and in the north porch.

Royal Coat of Arms of Charles II

with the Borough of Grantham arms below

Hatchment for Henry Pennant
1713 - 1772

Medieval chest used to store the church plate

The Common Hutch was used
to keep the Borough charters
and other important documents.

Memorials

There are nearly 70 memorials inside the church not counting the gravestones lying flat.

Harrington tomb c. 14th century

Richard Saltby tomb c. 14th century

Roll of Honour for those who fell in the First World War

1914 – 1919 REMEMBER WITH THANKSGIVING THE TRUE AND FAITHFUL MEN WHO IN THESE YEARS OF WAR WENT FORTH FROM THIS PLACE FOR GOD AND THE RIGHT · THE NAMES OF THOSE WHO RETURNED NOT AGAIN ARE HERE INSCRIBED TO BE HONOURED FOR EVERMORE · R·I·P

Sit Thomas Bury
died 4 May 1722

Capt. William Cust
KIA 8 March 1747

The sculptor was
Henry Cheere.

Tomb of Francis Malham of Elslacke - died 2 May 1660

Sir Dudley Ryder Memorial

He was Lord Chief Justice of the King's Bench. He was about to be created Baron of Harrowby but he died on 25 May 1756 before the Patent could pass.

The sculptor was Henry Cheere.

Edmund Turnor
died 5 January 1769

Church Silver

In 1808 the church silver was stolen from the chest installed in a niche in the crypt altar.

Pair of flagons (London 1809)
donated by Charles Clarke

From left to right:
Paten
Ciborium (London 1966) donated
        in memory of Ida Imber (1893 - 1970)
Lavabo (London 1821)

Top section of a processional cross
donated by the Confirmees 1896

Chalice (London 1915) - This was presented by the Manchester and Liverpool Pals of the 30th Division in 1916. It is also called the 'Tanner' Chalice as each soldier gave a tanner (6 pennies) towards the purchase of it.

Detail of the 'Pals' chalice

Organ

In 1640 Dr. Farmery presented an organ to the church, probably the first instrument to be installed. It was most likely destroyed at the time of the Civil War in 1643 by the Roundheads who used the woodwork for fuel.

In 1736, a new organ consisting of three manuals built by John Byfield was installed forming the core of today's instrument.

In 1869, as part of the Scott re-ordering of the church, the organ was rebuilt by Foster & Andrews and sited in its present position. The palatial oak case was designed by Sir Walter Tapper in 1906.

Then in 1950, as a result of damage caused by a leaking roof it was overhauled and re-voiced by Rushworth & Dreaper. In 1972, it was again re-built by Cousans of Lincoln.

A fourth manual was added and improvements to the electric action were made as part of the overhaul in 1993/4.

Organ case facing down the North aisle

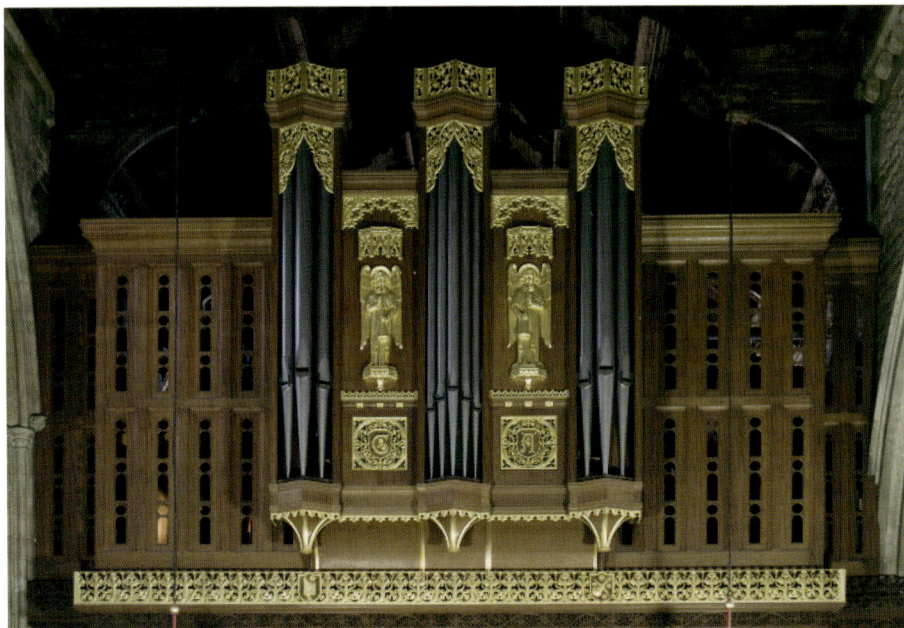

Organ case facing into the chancel
with a gilded angel trumpeter >

The four manual organ with
the Master of the Music
Dr Tim Williams in 2009

Bells

It is not known when the first peal of bells were hung in St. Wulfram's, but we do know that they were re-hung in 1640, and again in 1888 at a cost of £388.

The Ringing Chamber above the West door of St. Wulfram's

An article by Brian Buttery about the Ringing Chamber and the bells is reproduced on the next page.

The Ringing Chamber at Saint Wulfram's Church, Grantham is one of the largest and most attractive in the Lincoln Diocese. Despite the five feet thick walls of the tower the room is thirty feet square and contains much of interest and is found fifty feet up the tower; a climb of some 74 steps. It is of historic curiosity that the spiral staircase is anticlockwise and therefore requires a left handed swordsman to defend the tower.

There are many peal boards decorating the walls of the chamber which recount the peals rung on the bells since the late 1700s. Peals on the bells take over three and a half hours to ring and are usually to commemorate some special event. Each peal must be over 5000 changes. In the late 1800s when the church was restored the charity boards which hung in the church aisles were removed to the Ringing Chamber and relate to the grants and gifts to the church over many centuries. The most well-known one being "The Solomon Bequest" for an annual sermon to be preached against drunkenness (see 22 on p.46).

Other points of interest include several stone carvings, a set of hand bells, the rules of the society and the church clock mechanism dating from the 1860s. The clock is still in use but the winding mechanism has been electrified to save having to wind it each day.

The tower now contains 14 bells: the original peal of ten bells that were recast in 1946, two treble bells that were installed in 2003 and a further "Jubilee Bell" installed in 2013 to mark the Diamond Jubilee of Her Majesty Queen Elizabeth the Second. The 14th bell, the Sanctus Bell, is the oldest in the tower, dated 1674, and was cast in memory of the Revd. Hurst, Chaplain to Charles II and is referred to as "The Ting-Tang". It is rung prior to services in the church. The "Ting-Tang" is hung in the Green Chamber above the other 13 bells. All the bells were cast by John Taylor and Co. of Loughborough with the exception of the Sanctus Bell which was cast by Thomas Norris.

This gives us three rings of bells by using different combinations of bells:

- An original peal of 10 bells with a tenor weighing 32 cwt. 1 qtr. 11lbs. in C#
- A peal of 12 bells using the same tenor
- A peal of 8 bells with a tenor weigh 10 cwt. 1 qtr. 11 lbs. in G#

Since 1781, when the Society was founded, the bells have been rung by the members of the Saint Wulfram's Society of Change Ringers which is regarded as the oldest society in Grantham.

text by Brian Buttery

27. Two fine carvings with a Green Man on the right 30.

Legend would have it that this jug which holds 10 quarts (c. 11 litres) was used to carry beer to the bell ringers at the rate of 2 pints (c. 1 litre) per man.

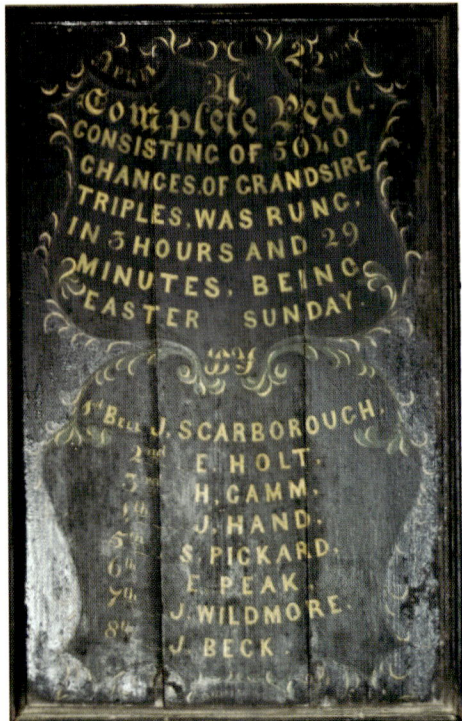

← 15. The earliest peal board 22 April 1764

Some peal boards record peals that mark special occasions.

16. This one was rung on the 20 June 1814 after the Treaty of Fontainebleau (11 April 1814) 'ended' the Napoleonic Wars and Napoleon was exiled to Elba.

It was not in fact the 'end' as Napoleon still had to escape from Elba and be defeated at Waterloo on 18 June 1815.

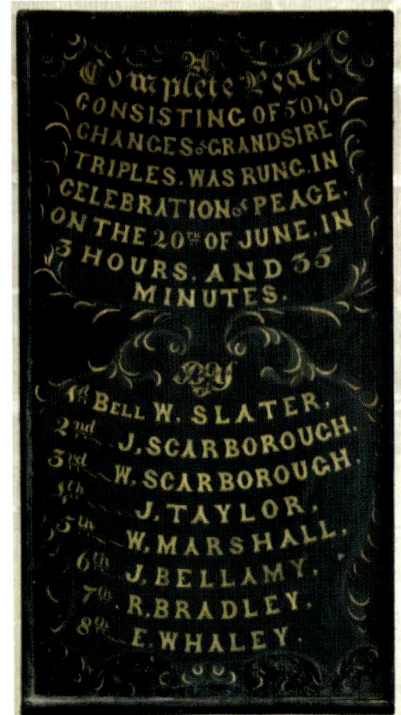

A Complete Peal CONSISTING OF 5040 CHANGES OF GRANDSIRE TRIPLES WAS RUNG IN 3 HOURS AND 29 MINUTES, BEING EASTER SUNDAY BY
1st Bell J. SCARBOROUGH,
2nd E. HOLT,
3rd H. CAMM,
4th J. HAND,
5th S. PICKARD,
6th E. PEAK,
7th J. WILDMORE,
8th J. BECK

A Complete Peal CONSISTING OF 5040 CHANGES OF GRANDSIRE TRIPLES WAS RUNG IN CELEBRATION OF PEACE ON THE 20th OF JUNE IN 3 HOURS AND 35 MINUTES BY
1st Bell W. SLATER,
2nd J. SCARBOROUGH,
3rd W. SCARBOROUGH,
4th J. TAYLOR,
5th W. MARSHALL,
6th J. BELLAMY,
7th R. BRADLEY,
8th E. WHALEY.

The old bells prior to recasting in 1946

The original tenor bell (No 13) prior to recasting in 1946

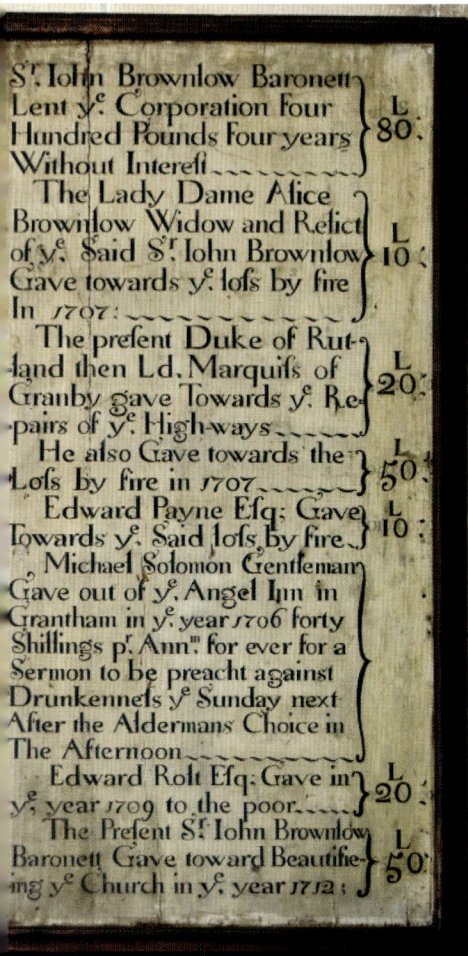

Sr. Iohn Brownlow Baronett
Lent yᵉ Corporation Four
Hundred Pounds Four years } L
80.
Without Interest
The Lady Dame Alice
Brownlow Widow and Relict
of yᵉ Said Sr. Iohn Brownlow } L
10
Gave towards yᵉ loss by fire
In 1707:
The present Duke of Rut-
land then Ld. Marquiss of } L
20
Granby gave Towards yᵉ Re-
pairs of yᵉ High-ways
He also Gave towards the } L
50
Loss by fire in 1707
Edward Payne Esq; Gave } L
10
Towards yᵉ Said loss by fire
Michael Solomon Gentleman
Gave out of yᵉ Angel Inn in
Grantham in yᵉ year 1706 forty
Shillings pr. Annm for ever for a
Sermon to be preacht against
Drunkenness yᵉ Sunday next
After the Aldermans Choice in
The Afternoon
Edward Rolt Esq; Gave in } L
20
yᵉ year 1709 to the poor
The Present Sr. Iohn Brownlow } L
50
Baronett Gave toward Beautifie-
ing yᵉ Church in yᵉ year 1712;

The bell mechanism above the Ringing Chamber

In the late 1800s the charity boards which had been hung in the church were moved to the Ringing Chamber.

22. a charity board including the 'Solomon bequest' from 1712

photo by Brian Buttery

2 treble bells (No 1 & 13) cast in 2003

photo by Brian Buttery

46

Index of books in the Francis Trigge Library referenced in this booklet

John Glenn and David Walsh privately published the 'Catalogue of the Francis Trigge Chained Library' in 1988. There were 356 entries in this catalogue.

In 2018 a digital version was created by John Manterfield and Roger Sleigh during the process of making a photographic record of each book cover and title page. This has 494 entries and does not replicate the bibliographic detail of the 1988 version. The index system used by Messrs Glenn & Walsh is continued through the digital catalogue and extended for the new acquisitions. The on line catalogue may be accessed on application to the Parish Clerk.

The books themselves are mostly stored on shelves labelled A to K. The list below uses the Glenn/Walsh index (extended) and gives the shelf and sequence position in [ ]. Some items are on display around the church and are identified with a P prefix. A few volumes are loose in the Library and are identified with an R prefix.